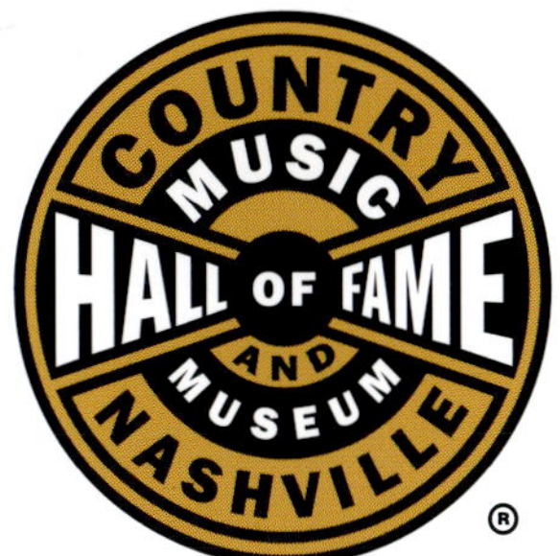

Dolly Parton

JOURNEY of a SEEKER

Country Music Foundation Press

222 Rep. John Lewis Way S · Nashville, Tennessee 37203

Published 2025. Printed in the United States of America.

978-0-915608-48-5

This publication was created by the staff of the Country Music Hall of Fame® and Museum.

Editor: Paul Kingsbury • Artifact photos by Bob Delevante • Printer: Lithographics, Inc., Nashville, Tennessee

On the cover: Dolly Parton in Joelton, Tennessee, December 1997. Cover photo © Jim Herrington

CONTENTS

Dolly in her tour bus, 1979. PHOTO BY RAEANNE RUBENSTEIN

INSIDE FRONT AND BACK COVER: Dolly's custom-designed patchwork blouse, worn at an Imagination Library program in Wilmington, Delaware, in 2022

Dolly in Nashville's Centennial Park, 1975. PHOTO BY RAEANNE RUBENSTEIN

DEAR MUSEUM FRIEND,

What can't she do? After accomplishing enough for three lifetimes, Dolly Parton continues to astound and amaze us. With her boundless talent. Her vivacious wit. And her tremendous generosity.

It's hard to believe that once upon a time she was a schoolgirl in East Tennessee and that she came from a family so needy that Dolly's mother had to piece together a coat from colorful rags to keep her from the cold. And when she wore it proudly to school, this future superstar was teased by the other children because of that patchwork coat.

Hard to believe that happened. But not impossible. Because Dolly wrote an achingly beautiful song describing that experience. "Coat of Many Colors" became a hit, and it has gone on to be recorded by more than sixty other artists, including Shania Twain with Alison Krauss, Sierra Ferrell, and Country Music Hall of Fame member Emmylou Harris.

Like all great artists, Dolly has demonstrated consistently that she can transform adversity and setbacks into works of stunning beauty and insight into the human condition. In our exhibit—*Dolly Parton: Journey of a Seeker*—we recount Dolly's story through a series of vignettes in which we see her overcome obstacles and know-it-all naysayers to achieve incredible feats of artistry, business success, and philanthropic generosity.

What we learn from these episodes is that Dolly's fame and financial success were not preordained. Things could have easily turned out differently for the girl from Locust Ridge, Tennessee, in spite of her immense talent. But she believed in herself, and she was determined from an early age to make music—and to make her mark in music. And so she did. Then, once she had begun to master those challenges, she kept looking for new tests of her abilities.

Each time, she broke new ground—as a songwriter, as a TV personality, as a film and TV actor, as a Hollywood producer, as the owner of one of the most popular theme parks in the world, as a leader in education and social uplift in the form of the Imagination Library for children, and more.

What can't she do? I can't answer that question. I don't think we've found out yet. But what *can* she do . . . that story is told in our exhibition and in the pages of this book.

Sincerely,

Kyle Young | CEO

ACKNOWLEDGMENTS

We hope this book and the exhibition it accompanies, *Dolly Parton: Journey of a Seeker*, convey the importance of Dolly Parton's many enduring accomplishments and good works. The book and exhibition are collaborations between Dolly, her representatives, and the Country Music Hall of Fame and Museum.

We are grateful to Dolly and others who have loaned artifacts and photographs, which help tell her inspiring life story and which aided the production of this book and the exhibition. Individuals who provided key assistance include John Zarling of Results Global; Danny Nozell, Olly Rowland, and Kelly Ridgway of CTK Enterprises; Rebecca Seaver, Christian Ferguson, and Steve Summers of Dolly Parton Enterprises; Eugene Naughton of Dollywood; Jeff Conyers and Tracy Long of the Dollywood Foundation; Marcel Pariseau of True Public Relations; Richie Owens; and Randy Fox.

Many museum staff members devoted time and talent to the book and the exhibit. Space prohibits listing them all, but some deserve mention here. Vice President of Museum Services Michael Gray and Executive Director of Exhibits and Curatorial Services John Sloboda led the curatorial team, which consisted of Michael McCall, Allison Moorer, Mick Buck, Kathleen Boyle, Shepherd Alligood, Kevin Fleming, Kathleen Campbell, Alan Stoker, Chris Fleming, Elek Horvath, Jack Clutter, Rosemary Zlokas, and Rachel Jacob. Executive Vice President of External Affairs Lisa Purcell, Senior Director of Editorial Paul Kingsbury, Vice President of Creative Services Warren Denney, Senior Director of Creative Luke Wiget, Creative Design Director Bret Pelizzari, Senior Graphic Designers Arlie Birket and Mills F.H. Penticoff, and project managers Cammy Harris and Whitney Waddell merit special recognition.

Dolly wore these red and silver platform mules, designed by Andreas, at the 2019 Grammy Awards.

Dolly, 1976. PHOTO FROM THE LEONARD KAMSLER COLLECTION OF THE COUNTRY MUSIC HALL OF FAME AND MUSEUM

BY MICHAEL McCALL AND ALLISON MOORER

Even among living legends, Dolly Parton's star shines with unusual brilliance. Her fame casts a wider, brighter light today than at any time in her career of sixty-plus years. It's inevitable in life that stars fade with time. But Dolly is an exception; she grows in stature and relevance each year. When divisions seem to deepen between us, Dolly prevails as a unifier, setting a standard for how to transform personal gain into a positive force in the world.

At this point, the scope of her talent and magnitude of her charisma could lead one to view her journey as a gilded fairytale and her path from impoverished mountain child to sparkling celebrity as predetermined and unstoppable. But that story would ignore the obstacles she overcame: how many times someone told her not to try something new, or warned that a goal was too risky, or that an idea would never work.

In truth, her achievements as an entertainer, a businesswoman, and a philanthropist required a determinaton to get past those who tried to limit the scale of her dreams. By always moving forward, Dolly Rebecca Parton succeeded beyond what anyone other than Dolly could have imagined.

I HAVE ALWAYS BEEN A SEEKER IN EVERY WAY. MY SPIRITUAL LIFE, MY PROFESSIONAL LIFE, MY PERSONAL LIFE. I'M ALWAYS LOOKING. I'M ALWAYS TRYING TO FIND ANOTHER MOUNTAIN TO CLIMB.

—DOLLY PARTON

DREAMS BEYOND the Mountains

On July 25, 1959, thirteen-year-old Dolly Parton made her Grand Ole Opry debut—even though an Opry manager refused to schedule her, citing her youth. Undeterred, Parton and her uncle Bill Owens persuaded singer Jimmy C. Newman to give Dolly one of his time slots. "I sang a George Jones song and got an encore," she recalled. "I thought, 'Boy, this is just great!' Then I got another encore. I thought that was even greater!" Her persistence established a pattern: Dolly would not let business-as-usual policies discourage the pursuit of her dreams.

Born January 19, 1946, the fourth of twelve children, Dolly grew up on Locust Ridge, fifteen miles east of Sevierville in the Smoky Mountains of Tennessee. The family lived in a remote four-room cabin with no plumbing or electricity. Despite limited opportunities, Dolly embraced her father's enterprising work ethic and her mother's love of traditional Scots-Irish folk music to pursue her dream of becoming an entertainer.

Dolly, three years old, Sevier County, Tennessee

I BELIEVE YOU CAN MAKE YOUR DREAMS COME TRUE TO A BIG DEGREE, DON'T YOU? I WON'T ACCEPT ANYTHING ELSE.

—DOLLY PARTON
TO JOURNALIST CHET FLIPPO

This c. 1964 demo of Dolly singing a previously unknown pop song was recently found in the collections of the Country Music Hall of Fame and Museum.

BELOW: Dolly's first single, "Puppy Love," released April 20, 1959. Though credited to Bill Owens, Dolly's uncle, Dolly wrote the song at age eleven.

OPPOSITE PAGE:
Dolly, nine years old.
PHOTO FROM THE *MUSIC CITY NEWS* COLLECTION OF THE COUNTRY MUSIC HALL OF FAME AND MUSEUM

"This was a lifelong plan," Dolly said. "From the time I was little I loved music. Then, I learned there was this place you could go to become a star. I always wanted to be a star. I wanted to do something with music, but I always wanted that glamourous way of life."

She started right away to make her dreams a reality. At age ten, Dolly performed regularly on Knoxville radio and TV shows; at thirteen, she recorded teen-pop tunes in Louisiana for Goldband Records; at sixteen, she signed with Mercury Records in Nashville. She moved there to begin her career in earnest the day after finishing high school, May 30, 1964.

A SMART *Blonde*

As she continued to impress Nashville music executives with her singing talent, Dolly Parton confronted another barrier. Although she considered herself a country singer, record producers saw an opportunity for her to follow young Nashville sensations Brenda Lee and the Everly Brothers into the booming teen-pop market.

Dolly tried. Signing in 1965 with Monument Records, her third record label by age nineteen, she initially recorded pop and rockabilly songs. Then Monument label owner Fred Foster heard "Put It Off Until Tomorrow," a song Dolly co-wrote with her uncle Bill Owens that became a Top Ten country hit by singer Bill Phillips.

Publicity photo for Monument Records, c. 1965

Dolly's key ring
from the 1960s

"

WE ALWAYS MADE A JOKE THAT ME AND MY UNCLE HAD REAL BAD SINUS TROUBLE WHEN WE WENT TO NASHVILLE. WE WENT TO EVERY LABEL IN TOWN, AND NOBODY WOULD SIGN . . . US.

—DOLLY PARTON
TO JOURNALIST CHET FLIPPO

Recognizing Dolly's strengths—including her uncredited harmony vocals on the recording—Foster produced the traditional-leaning *Hello, I'm Dolly*. Released in 1967, the album included her first country hits, "Dumb Blonde" and "Something Fishy," the latter of which she wrote.

That year, Dolly and uncles Bill and Louis Owens formed Owe-Par Publishing, a savvy business decision for a twenty-one-year-old that resulted in Dolly earning a larger percentage of her song royalties. It was a move that helped create her fortune.

Souvenirs from an awards night: BMI Country Award Dinner program, invitation, and place cards, 1966

LEFT: Dolly wore this 1960s sheath dress, designed by Lucy Adams, on the cover of her first album *Hello, I'm Dolly*, released by Monument Records in 1967.

RCA VICTOR

HEY, *Porter*

With Dolly Parton's career gaining momentum, a surprise offer from country star Porter Wagoner presented a difficult choice. "When I got called to go into Porter's office, I thought he was going to cut some of my songs," Dolly recalled of her meeting with Wagoner in the summer of 1967. "I didn't know Norma Jean was leaving." Norma Jean Beasler had been the female star in Porter Wagoner's act since 1960. But she had decided to leave Wagoner, and the Opry star had an opening in his show to fill.

The question for Dolly was: should she continue to build her solo career, or join Wagoner as his musical partner on records, on tour, and on his popular syndicated TV series? The TV show would give Dolly more national exposure. However, it also meant she would record fewer of her own songs and relinquish control of her career.

Porter Wagoner and Dolly recording at RCA Studio B, late 1960s

Dolly agreed to join Wagoner's act and made her first appearance on *The Porter Wagoner Show* in September 1967. Despite initial backlash from Norma Jean's fans, the TV show became even more popular. Porter and Dolly recorded thirteen albums together, with eleven reaching the *Billboard* country Top Ten. Fourteen of their singles, including "The Last Thing on My Mind" and "Just Someone I Used to Know," were Top Ten country hits. Their vocal duets won three Country Music Association awards and an Academy of Country Music award.

OPPOSITE PAGE: This is the yellow dress that Dolly wore on the cover of the duet album *Porter 'n' Dolly* (pictured above), released on RCA Victor Records in 1974. The dress was designed by Lucy Adams.

RIGHT: Silver glitter block heel Mary Janes, designed by Mary Lou Fashions. Dolly wore these on *The Porter Wagoner Show*.

Porter Wagoner and Dolly appeared in Kansas City for two shows on March 26, 1972.

Songteller

After becoming Porter Wagoner's duet partner in 1967, Dolly Parton initially struggled to score solo hits. While the duo became regulars on country radio, Dolly failed to break through on her own. Her first four RCA albums generated only six singles. "Just Because I'm a Woman" fared best at #17 on the country singles chart.

But she persisted. A new decade opened with Dolly's first solo Top Ten, a spirited take on the Jimmie Rodgers classic "Mule Skinner Blues." She followed it with her first #1, "Joshua," a song she was inspired to write by the rugged men she knew who lived deep in the Appalachian woods.

"I think it's just natural to write songs if you're brought up that way," she said. "It's a way to put all your feelings and emotions down, and I had a gift of rhyme and I loved to think stuff. As long as I can remember, I remember writing songs . . . I think it's just a gift that's been handed down in my family for generations."

RCA Victor Records publicity photo, mid-1970s. PHOTO BY BOB SCHANZ STUDIO

HOLIDAY LAKE PARK

SPARTANBURG, S.C.

SUN. NOV. 2

3 P.M. TILL 10 FREE RIDES FOR KIDS

Gate Price Tickets $6, Children Under 12 Free

Advance Tickets From Any Hillbilly Unit of Shriners

GRAND OLE OPRY®

PRESENTS - IN PERSON

DOLLY PARTON

AND HER

FAMILY TRAVELING BAND

REPRINTED FROM THE ORIGINAL PLATES COPYRIGHT 1994 HATCH SHOW PRINT HAND MADE QUALITY POSTERS SINCE 1879

Dolly noticed how fans responded to narrative tales about growing up poor in Appalachia. She refocused her songwriting and hit her stride with a series of hits drawing on personal experiences and observations. "Coat of Many Colors," "My Tennessee Mountain Home," and "The Bargain Store" all became Top Twenty country hits. "I naturally, when I first left home, was homesick so I wrote a lot of songs about home," she recalled. "So that I could carry it with me." Her songs of love and love's challenges—"I Will Always Love You," "Jolene," and "Love Is Like a Butterfly"—brought new dimensions to a common subject. All three of these became #1 country hits in 1974. That was also the year she left Wagoner's act to take control of her own destiny.

RIGHT: Custom Gibson banjo with inlaid butterflies. Dolly played this banjo on tour in 1992 and on her *Halos and Horns* tour in 2002.

TOP: 1971 Sony TC-110A cassette tape recorder. Dolly wrote "I Will Always Love You," "Jolene," and "The Seeker" using this machine.

OPPOSITE PAGE: Blue pantsuit with multi-colored rhinestone flower detailing, c. 1975, designed by Lucy Adams

This Hatch Show Print poster promoted an appearance by Dolly Parton and her Traveling Family Band in Spartanburg, South Carolina, November 2, 1975. She formed the group, which included her sisters Rachel and Frieda, her brothers Floyd and Randy, and her uncles and cousins, after parting ways with Porter Wagoner in 1974.

THE STORY BEHIND "Jolene"

"The name Jolene I got from a little girl that had come to a show one night back when I was with Porter. And she'd had pictures made in her little Girl Scout outfit, and I could tell she was real proud of the fact that she was a Girl Scout. So she brought a picture for me and one for Porter and on the back it said, 'To Miss Dolly, Love Jolene' and the other one said, 'To Porter, Love Jolene.' And I thought, 'Boy, what a beautiful name!' I'd never heard that name. And I made comment, I said, 'I bet you're named after your Daddy.' And she said, 'No, Jolene's just my name.' I thought her Daddy's name was Joe like an Earline or whatever. I just kept thinking 'What a pretty name.' And for weeks after that I kept saying Jolene. If I ever have a little girl I'm going to name her Jolene. So I just kept saying, 'Jolene, Jolene, Jolene.' So one night I was just in the kitchen piddling around cooking or something, and I just kept singing, 'Jolene, Jolene, Jolene, Jolene.' [pause] 'Jolene, Jolene, Jolene, Jolene.' So then I just got this big, wild idea that I couldn't think of a way that I could write a song about a woman that I could sing. But I wanted to sing it myself 'cause I liked the name. So I just made up that story."

—DOLLY PARTON TO JOURNALIST CHET FLIPPO

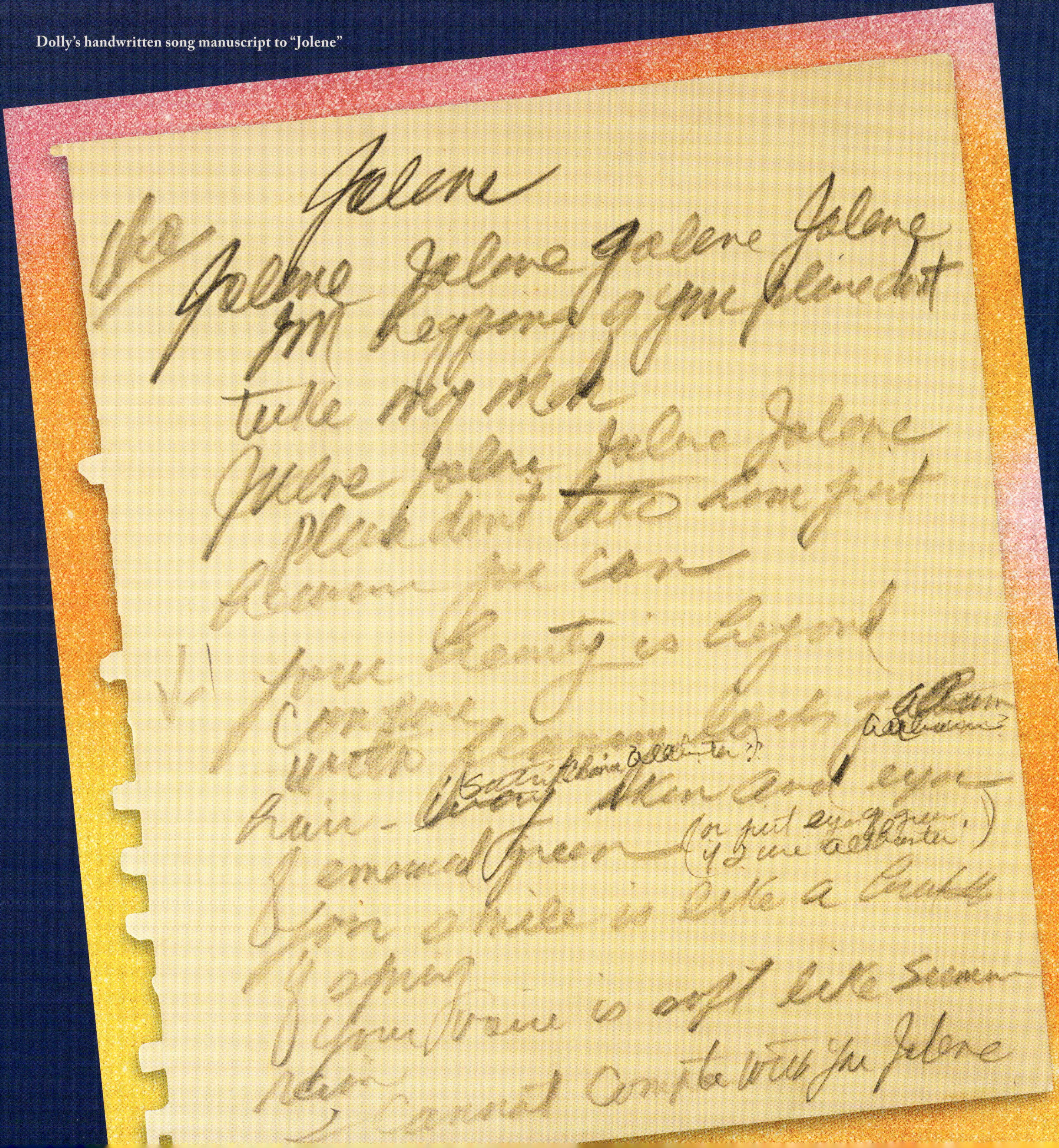

Dolly's handwritten song manuscript to "Jolene"

Jolene

Ch
Jolene Jolene Jolene Jolene
I'm begging of you please don't
take my man
Jolene Jolene Jolene Jolene
please don't ~~take~~ take him just
because you can

V-1
Your beauty is beyond
compare
with flaming locks of auburn
hair - (Satin, Chin, Alabaster?) ~~ivory~~ skin and eyes
of emerald green (or just eyes of green if I use alabaster)
Your smile is like a breath
of spring
Your voice is soft like summer
rain
I cannot compete with you Jolene

ALL HER *Colors*

Dolly Parton's signature visual style emerged when she was a young girl growing up with a vivid imagination in the backwoods of East Tennessee. Instinctively drawn to colorful, shape-hugging clothing designs, Dolly exhibited a sartorial imagination born from her desire to stand apart and experience life beyond the Smoky Mountains. "It's a country girl's idea of glam," she said. "The way I look is the way I think I look the best, according to my rules and my personality."

After establishing herself in Nashville, Dolly resisted advice from record executives who warned that her flamboyant fashions would overshadow her talent. She was determined to present herself as boldly as she dreamed. She insisted on working with clothing designers and hair and makeup artists who would create performance looks that were tailored to her sense of style. They balanced utilitarian function with her personal ideals of glamour, the visions that first inspired her dreams of stardom.

Dolly, 1978. PHOTO BY HARRY LANGDON JR.

"When I started doing the pop stuff, they always tried to get me to wear more stylish, more fashionable, more tasteful clothes," she recalled. "But I said, 'Look, I'm gonna be me because I know who I am and you don't.' . . . I have to be comfortable in how I dress, how I see myself, and how I feel in what I'm wearing." Dolly draws considerable power from her one-of-a-kind wardrobe. Inseparable from her iconic image, each costume is an integral part of her creative expression.

Handed-beaded yellow and silver dress with beaded fringe, designed by Tony Chase. Dolly wore this for the CMA's thirty-fifth anniversary TV show, *A Country Celebration*, January 1993.
Design sketch by Tony Chase

OPPOSITE PAGE: Blue dress with silver beading and rhinestones, designed by Robért Behar. Dolly wore this dress on the *Backwoods Barbie Tour* at O2 Arena, London, England, 2008.
Design sketch by Robért Behar

Yellow high-low dress with purple overlay and pink slip, designed by Robért Behar. Dolly wore this dress in the video for "I'm Gone," 2003. Design sketch by Robért Behar

OPPOSITE PAGE: Nail extensions and artificial eyelashes that Dolly uses.

Design sketch by Robért Behar for the black and white embroidered and hand-beaded velvet and chiffon gown Dolly wore to the 2006 Kennedy Center Honorees' State Dinner.

Design sketch by Tony Chase for the blue, leopard print, hand-beaded wrap dress Dolly wore when she starred in the 1991 made-for-TV movie *Wild Texas Wind*.

Eve-N-Tips
The Nail People
Dragon Lady Nail Tips
Beautiful Nails
at a moments notice
NU-NAILS
SMALL
WITH HALF MOONS GLUE INSIDE BOX
ARTIFICIAL FINGER NAILS
be a lady to your finger tips
Fantasia
Christina's
HUMAN HAIR LASHES
WASH-N-WEAR
ANDREA

10/06
Dolly

bead a piece of hair band
bone
maybe feathers black & white
Dolly 3/91

Crossing OVER

When Dolly Parton signed with top Los Angeles talent manager Sandy Gallin of the Katz, Gallin & Cleary management firm in 1976 and collaborated with L.A. pop producer Gary Klein for her 1977 album *Here You Come Again*, many in the Nashville community accused her of abandoning country music in search of pop success.

But the ambitious East Tennessee native wanted to see how far her talent could take her. "I felt like God wanted me to be more," she said, "and to do more, and to get out and do my own thing."

Here You Come Again—with the title song going #1 country and #3 pop—became Dolly's first million-selling album and earned Dolly her first Grammy Award. From 1977 to 1980, she scored eight Top Ten country hits, seven of them reaching #1. Meanwhile, hits like "Two Doors Down" and "Baby I'm Burning" kept her music on the pop charts as well.

Dolly and Kenny Rogers when they performed "Islands in the Stream" at the 1983 CMA Awards

I ALWAYS SAID THAT MY DESIRE TO DO SOMETHING HAS BEEN GREATER THAN MY FEAR OF IT. AND THAT'S HOW I LIKE TO LIVE TODAY.

—DOLLY PARTON

"Everybody said I was making a big mistake leaving *The Porter Wagoner Show*," she recalled. "And when I said I wanted to do movies, I wanted to do bigger things, I wanted to have some crossover records, people said I was making a mistake. People said, 'You should never leave country.' I said, 'How in the world could I ever leave country? It's such a part of me I just take it with me wherever I go.'"

Hand-painted dress, designed by Patric Reeves-Aaron and worn by Dolly on *The Tonight Show* and in concert, 1979

TOP: Carol Burnett and Dolly at the press conference for the *Dolly & Carol in Nashville* TV special, 1979

OPPOSITE PAGE: Cover girl—*People*, 1977; *Playboy*, 1978; and *Rolling Stone*, 1980

THE STORY BEHIND "9 to 5"

"That was a song I wrote for the movie *9 to 5*. I was inspired just by what the story was about. But I purposely wrote that song, tried to work on it on the set every day, inspired by things that I would pick up and feel because it was all about the girls [in the film].

"In fact, the typewriter sound, I wrote that using my fingernails. [She demonstrates by clicking her fingernails together.] I had a guitar in my dressing room. I would sometimes go in at lunch and work it up. I would just do little things and make this sound [clicking her fingernails] where it would kind of sound like a typewriter. And I'd go [singing], 'I tumble out of bed and stumble in the kitchen. And pour myself a cup of ambition.' Then as I would write it, I would sing it to the girls on the set, and get everybody excited. So I kind of pulled from everybody.

"And then when I recorded it, I brought all the girls down, all the people that were on the set, and the producers—all the women—because it was about women's lib at the time, or just women in the workplace. So all the girls were singing on it, on the real record. We had Jane Fonda and Lily Tomlin, and all the secretaries, all the actors, and all the girls who worked in the production offices. So it kind of was our song. I included everybody in that one, and I did that on purpose because I wanted it to be born there, on the set."

—DOLLY PARTON

Dolly receiving gold record awards for her "9 to 5" single and album, 1980.
FROM LEFT: RCA Nashville VP Jerry Bradley, Dolly, her record producer Gregg Perry, RCA President Robert Summer, RCA Nashville VP of Marketing Joe Galante, and RCA Nashville Director of Sales and Promotion Dave Wheeler.

Screen Gem

When Jane Fonda heard Dolly Parton's 1978 hit "Two Doors Down," she immediately associated Dolly's expressive southern voice with a key character in her upcoming film, *9 to 5*, released in 1980. "Trying to change my accent would've been a really hard thing to do," Dolly said, looking back. "I'd been offered lots of films, but it was only when I got the *9 to 5* script that I thought, 'Well, I can play that.'" Stepping into the part of Doralee Rhodes, Dolly proved to be as charismatic on film as she was on stage and TV. Film critic Roger Ebert called her "a natural-born movie star."

She soon moved easily into starring roles in *The Best Little Whorehouse in Texas* (1982) with Burt Reynolds, *Rhinestone* (1984) with Sylvester Stallone, *Steel Magnolias* (1989) with an all-star cast that included Sally Field and Shirley MacLaine, and *Straight Talk* (1992) with James Woods.

Dolly at a press conference for the movie *9 to 5*, 1980

BELOW: *9 to 5* cast gift

RIGHT: promo photo of cast—Jane Fonda, Lily Tomlin, Dolly, and Dabney Coleman

OPPOSITE PAGE: Dolly's cowgirl dress from *9 to 5*

Sheet music cover for Dolly's song "Tennessee Homesick Blues," a #1 country hit from the soundtrack of the movie *Rhinestone* (1984)

TV continued to be a significant vehicle for her. She hosted her own variety series in two different decades and became the go-to host for several country music specials on various networks. She teamed with established TV star Carol Burnett as co-host of *Dolly & Carol in Nashville* (1979) and took on acting roles in TV comedies and dramas. She became a fan favorite in a recurring role on the Disney Channel's *Hannah Montana* (2006–2011), and Johnny Carson, the star-making host of *The Tonight Show*, invited her on his show twenty-five times.

FROM LEFT: **Shirley MacLaine, Daryl Hannah, Sally Field, Dolly, and Julia Roberts attend the premiere of *Steel Magnolias*, 1989.**
PHOTO: MICHAEL OCHS/GETTY

CLOCKWISE FROM TOP LEFT:

Poster for *The Best Little Whorehouse in Texas* and script for the 1982 movie

Black pumps by Allure that Dolly wore in the movie *Straight Talk*, 1992

Broadway ticket keychain engraved "Love from Burt," given to Dolly by her co-star Burt Reynolds

Dollywood

When Dolly Parton considered investing in a theme park in her native Smoky Mountains, a chorus of advisers warned against it. For twenty-five years, a string of attractions in a promising location failed to hold the public's attention. In 1961, a Civil War–themed village in Pigeon Forge, Tennessee, had offered rides on a passenger train pulled by a steam-powered locomotive. That attraction eventually evolved into a park called Silver Dollar City.

Where others saw a minor point of local interest, Dolly saw potential. She believed in the lure of the scenic Smokies and felt that emphasizing music, food, and family fun would increase attendance. In 1986, in partnership with Herschend Family Entertainment, she opened Dollywood on the site of Silver Dollar City, offering a mix of cutting-edge thrill rides, downhome entertainment, and natural beauty.

Dolly at the opening of Dollywood, 1986

come To
HOMESPUN

"Every time I'd go to Hollywood, I'd see that sign and thought if I just changed that *H* to a *D*, that would be Dollywood," she recalled. "A lot of my business people at the time thought I was making a big mistake to invest money and time [in a theme park], so I got rid of them and got new accountants, new lawyers that believed in what I was doing. And evidently it's worked out okay 'cause now it's one of the biggest parks in the whole world and I'm very proud of that."

In its first year, more than a million visitors filled the park. Now 165 acres, Dollywood draws three million visitors annually and includes two resort lodges, a water park, three themed dinner shows, a comedy barn, and other activities. Today it's one of the top attractions in Tennessee and the largest employer in Sevier County.

LEFT: White, red, blue, green, and silver hand-beaded dress, designed by Ann Roth. Dolly wore this for the *Dolly in London* concert special in 1983 and at Dollywood.

People cover, 1986

OPPOSITE PAGE: Early Dollywood brochures

very kid can play and dream at 'Critter Creek Playland'

AN *Eagle* WHEN SHE *Flies*

RCA Records shocked the music world when the label dropped Dolly Parton, Charley Pride, and Waylon Jennings from its roster in 1986, as the label moved to invest in new talent. Nevertheless, Dolly remained a star on country radio, with two #1s released in 1985, including "Real Love," her second #1 hit with Kenny Rogers after "Islands in the Stream" in 1983. But she hadn't earned a gold album since *9 to 5 and Odd Jobs* was certified in 1981.

Dolly, Emmylou Harris, and Linda Ronstadt, in a publicity photo for their 1987 album *Trio*

A Christmas to Remember

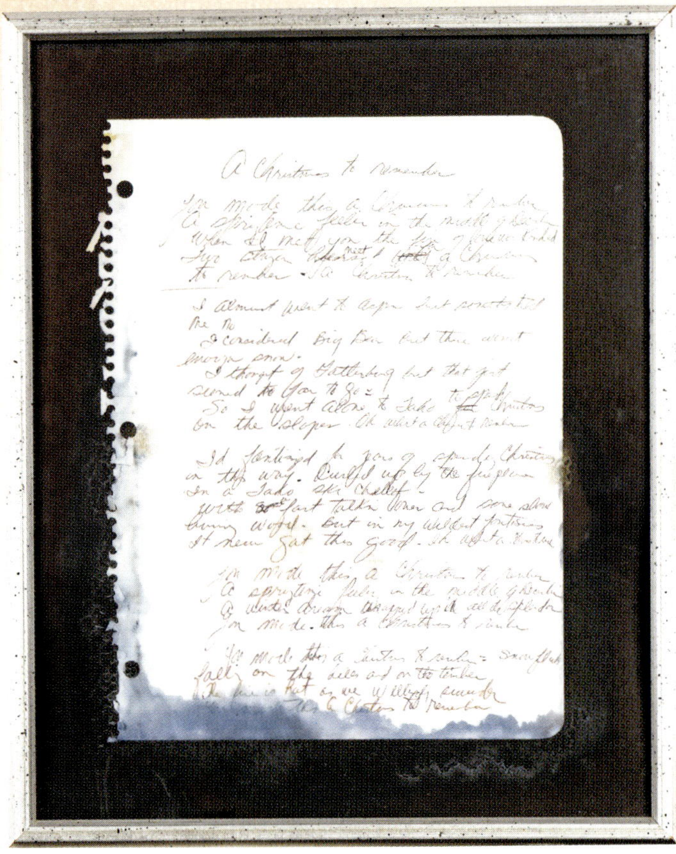

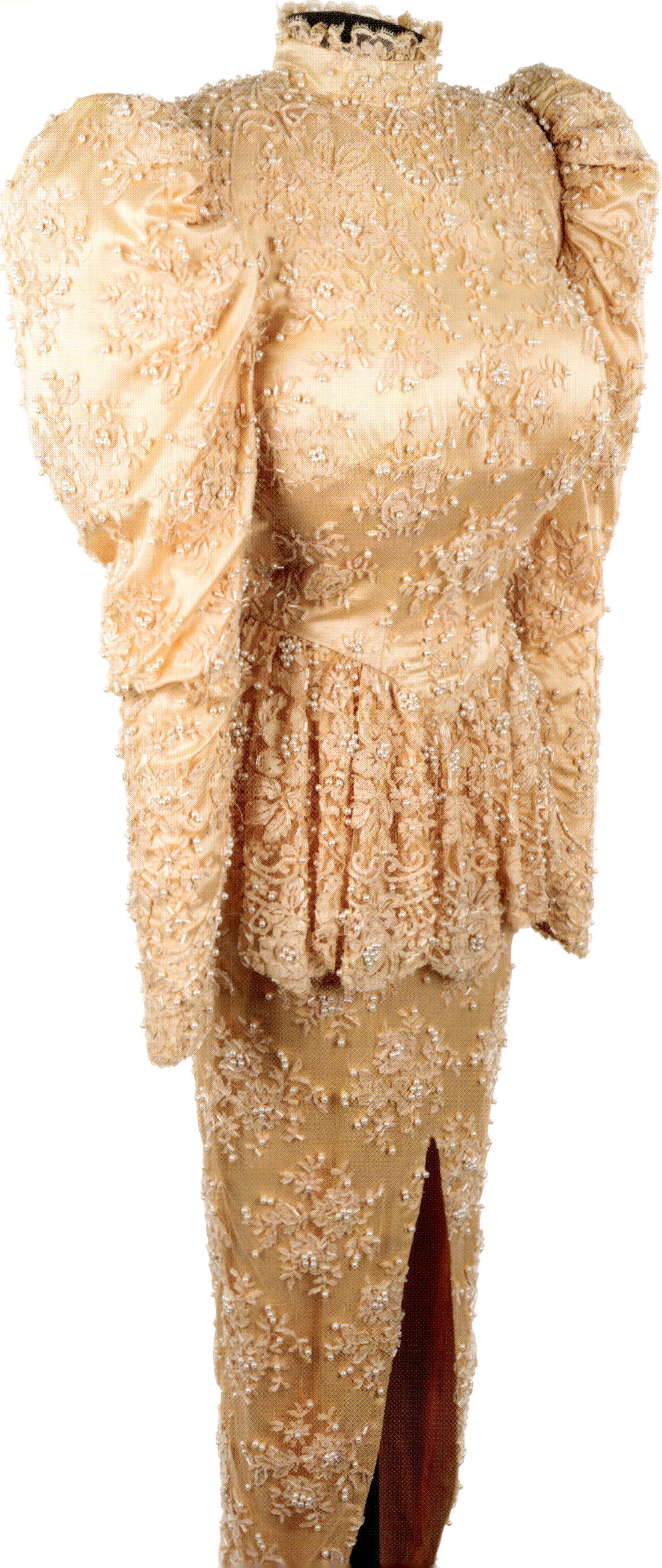

Dolly responded in 1987 with *Trio*, a Grammy-winning collaboration with Emmylou Harris and Linda Ronstadt that had a traditional folk-country sound. Next, Dolly signed with Columbia Records, teaming with hot producer Ricky Skaggs in 1989 to create the album *White Limozeen*, which included two #1 hits, including "Why'd You Come in Here Looking Like That." The album sold more than a half-million copies, her first solo gold record since *9 to 5*. Three more gold-selling albums followed, with the platinum sales of *Eagle When She Flies* (1991) driven by "Rockin' Years," her hit duet with Ricky Van Shelton that was written by her brother Floyd.

RIGHT: **Black satin bomber-style jacket embroidered with Dolly's name, the words "Queenston Trio," and four queen cards. The back is embroidered with roses and the word "Trio," 1986.**

BOTTOM RIGHT: **The Grammy for Best Country Performance by a Duo or Group, which was won by Dolly, Emmylou Harris, and Linda Ronstadt for *Trio***

BELOW: **Promotional poster for the *Trio* album**

OPPOSITE PAGE: **Handwritten lyrics by Dolly for "A Christmas to Remember"**

Peach lace peplum dress with pearls and hand-beading. Dolly wore this on her *Dolly* TV show when she sang with Miss Piggy, 1987.

Sandollar
PRODUCTIONS

The high financial risks of producing multimillion-dollar films have stripped fortunes from many investors, including actors. When Dolly launched Sandollar Productions in 1986 with manager Sandy Gallin, the combination of her inexperience as a Hollywood producer and the typical failure rate of small film companies led to dire predictions.

The company started with *A Smoky Mountain Christmas* (1986), a made-for-TV holiday film with Dolly in the starring role. The company earned further respect with the groundbreaking *Common Threads: Stories from the Quilt* (1989) about the Names Project Memorial AIDS Quilt. The film won an Academy Award for Best Documentary Feature. Other Sandollar hits included the Steve Martin comedy

Dolly with longtime manager and business partner Sandy Gallin, 1993. PHOTO BY JIM SMEAL/GETTY

I'M PREPARED FOR SUCCESS, AND BRAVE FOR FAILURE.

—DOLLY PARTON
TO JOURNALIST CHET FLIPPO

Dolly Parton

Dear Dolly —
Peace of mind,
Happiness, Health and
never change!!!
With love Sandy

Father of the Bride (1991), the long-running TV series *Buffy the Vampire Slayer* (1997–2003), and the romantic remake of *Sabrina* (1995) with Harrison Ford.

After Gallin retired, Dolly opened her own film company, Southern Light. It evolved into Dixie-Pixie Productions, which created films with Warner Bros. and teamed with Magnolia Hill for an eight-part Netflix series with each episode inspired by a Dolly hit.

FATHER OF THE BRIDE
TriStar Pictures

Sandollar recently acquired the remake rights to the 1950 MGM classic FATHER OF THE BRIDE starring Spencer Tracy and Elizabeth Taylor. The producers and TriStar Pictures plan to turn the project into a vehicle for Jack Nicholson who will play a grown-up member of the counter-culture, now firmly entrenched in the middle class. When he learns he has to give up his precious daughter in marriage, it turns his household upside down and throws his own marriage and values into question. Actress Cindy Williams is Sandollar's producing partner.

THE WAR AT HOME
Writer: John Byrum
Director: John Byrum
Cast: Linda Fiorentino

THE WAR AT HOME is the story of Edie Sedgwick and Andy Warhol. The film will star Linda Fiorentino as Edie and Tom Hulce as Warhol. Not yet cast is the part of Terry, a fictional character. He is a working class guy hired to drive a car and make sure Edie arrives at the set on time. Gradually these two fall in love as Terry tries to save her from self-destruction. It is through Terry's eyes that we see the glamorous and decadent New York pop scene of the early 60's. Michael Taylor and Harvey Klaris are Sandollar's financial partners on the project which will be financed independently. John Byrum's credits include HEARTBEATS, INSERTS, and THE RAZOR'S EDGE.

Blue, hand-beaded, leopard-print wrap dress, which Dolly wore when she starred in the 1991 made-for-TV movie *Wild Texas Wind*. The dress was designed by Tony Chase.

RIGHT: Sandollar Productions project booklet

OPPOSITE PAGE: Note from Sandy Gallin to Dolly

THE STORY BEHIND

"Coat of Many Colors"

"I've written thousands of songs. I've had hundreds of them published, and I've recorded bunches of them. And I like different ones for different reasons. Some of them I like more as a singer, whereas some songs—like an 'I Will Always Love You'—are a great song to sing. That song says a lot, and you feel it, and you sing it. But I have to say of all the songs that I have written 'Coat of Many Colors' is my favorite one. Because it is more about an attitude, more about a philosophy of life.

"It talks more about the parents, your family, and the things that they tried to teach you. We were as poor as anybody could be. And Mama still had time to tell me a story from the Bible, to give me some sort of pride in wearing a ragged little coat made out of a bunch of scraps. She read me the story of Joseph and his coat of many colors—I know now—in order to give me some sort of pride because I'm sure she knew that I'd get laughed at in school for wearing that coat, which was just a piece of rags. But when I went home crying about it she also told me, 'We're not poor. Look around you. There's a lot of people living in this holler, and they can't even feed their kids. At least we're going to bed at night fed. And we got love, and we've got understanding and all the stuff that money can't buy.' I never sing that song that I don't see my whole life pass before me as a child."

—DOLLY PARTON

Parton family portrait, c. 1960. FRONT ROW: **Stella, Avie Lee with Rachel on her lap, Robert Lee, Cassie.** BACK ROW: **Randy, Dolly, Willadeene, Denver, Floyd, Bobby, Frieda, David.**

Celebrate the colorful
variety of feelings we all share
with the legendary
Dolly Parton!
Dolly Parton
I Am a
RAINBOW

Imagination LIBRARY

Robert Lee Parton, Dolly's father, grew up when Appalachian children went to work instead of classrooms. Because he never learned to read, he insisted that his children become readers. To honor her father, and to encourage an interest in reading in children age five and under in Sevier County, Dolly founded the Imagination Library in 1995. She shocked skeptics when 1,700 books reached mailboxes from the first month on.

In 1988, the singer launched the Dollywood Foundation, and the Imagination Library became its flagship program. In 2000, Dolly expressed her goal of taking the program to all fifty states. No way, the skeptics said. Too many books, too much territory.

Dolly launched the Imagination Library in 1995 to encourage a love of books and reading in children.

Dolly began by teaming with local public, private, and civic organizations across the country to fund and enable the expansion of the program. Today, the Imagination Library is active in all fifty states. But Dolly didn't stop there. Canada began participating in 2006, the UK in 2007, Australia in 2013, and Ireland in 2019. In 2025, the Imagination Library plans to deliver more than three million books.

"The Imagination Library is one of the greatest things I think I've done and ever will do," she said. "I think I'll be remembered as much for that as anything that I've ever done, even with my music, and I'm proud of it."

RIGHT: Orange skirt suit with gold embroidery, designed by Ruth. Dolly wore this at an Imagination Library event in 1998.

BELOW: A thank you note from a child to Dolly

OPPOSITE PAGE: Some of the many books distributed to families by the Imagination Library

DEAR DOLLY,
I LOVE YOUR SONG
9 TO 5. IT IS MY FAV-
ORITE. I LOVE YOU
DOLLY. CAN I BE YOUR
FRIEND DOLLY?

FROM: MIA.
TO: DOLLY

Llama llama red pajama
Anna Dewdney
Home for a Bunny
The Very Hungry Caterpillar's
FIRST
Somewhere, Right Now
BY KERRY DOCHERTY
PICTURES BY SUZIE MASON
A NEW YORK TIMES BESTSELLER
Hair Love
LITTLE ENGINE THAT COULD
The Very Hungry Caterpillar
EATS BREAKFAST
a COUNTING book
DOLLY PARTON
COAT OF MANY COLORS
EL ABRIGO DE MUCHOS COLORES
illustrated by | ilustrado por Brooke Boynton-Hughes
translated by | traducido por Teresa Mlawer

BLUE *Mountain Return*

By the late 1990s, Dolly Parton disciples the Chicks and Shania Twain ranked among popular music's highest-flying acts, selling albums in the multimillions and realizing Dolly's ambitions for pop-country success that began two decades earlier. It was at this juncture that Dolly chose to turn away from pop-country and record an album inspired by the mountain songs her mother played for her as a child. The decision showed just how willing she was to go against the grain while following her heart.

Dolly at singer-songwriter Jim Lauderdale's house, 2014. PHOTO BY DAVID McCLISTER

I ALWAYS LOVED BLUEGRASS MUSIC AND WAS MAKING A LIVING DOING A LOT OF OTHER THINGS AT THAT TIME. SO I THOUGHT, 'WELL, I HAD TO GET RICH TO SING LIKE I WAS POOR AGAIN.'

—DOLLY PARTON

Working with Sugar Hill Records, Dolly recorded a series of bluegrass and mountain music albums—*The Grass Is Blue, Little Sparrow,* and *Halos & Horns*—that turned a creative gambit into an unexpected success that briefly pushed bluegrass to the forefront of American culture. Working with young bluegrass stars, including Alison Krauss and Chris Thile, Dolly drew a surge of media attention. She won a Grammy for Best Bluegrass Album for *The Grass Is Blue* and another Grammy for Best Female Country Vocal Performance for "Shine," a bluegrass rendition of a Collective Soul song from *Little Sparrow*.

Blue velvet fringe wrap with gold hand-beading, rhinestones, and the title of her 1999 bluegrass album *The Grass Is Blue* embroidered on it

LEFT: Blue leather, hand-painted boots, designed by Bambi Breakstone and worn by Dolly in 2002

OPPOSITE PAGE: Dolly, 2000. PHOTO BY JIM HERRINGTON

Parton Family DNA

Dolly Parton has always credited the voice and guitar of her mother, Avie Lee Owens Parton, for her love of music, and her mother's brothers, Louis and Bill Owens, for providing crucial help early in her career. The interlocking stories of the Parton and Owens families extend back generations. Those rich musical stories continue today through a 2024 album, *Smoky Mountain DNA*, featuring Dolly performing with various members of her family.

Dolly and her mother, Avie Lee Parton

The album gives a full picture of the music Dolly grew up with and the important role music has played from her childhood until now. Across thirty-seven tracks, the album features the music of nine of her siblings and her aunts and uncles, and it highlights the varied musical directions the Parton and Owens families have taken through the decades. Richie Owens, son of Louis Owens and cousin to Dolly, compiled and produced the family album.

Dolly has always made clear how the music she heard from her extended family sustained and gave her direction. This is the music that shaped her, and the sounds of a family as its members weave their way through generations of influences.

Gibson L-30 acoustic archtop guitar, a gift to Dolly from Floyd Parton, her brother

OPPOSITE PAGE: Dolly's maternal grandfather, Rev. Jake Owens, was a Pentecostal preacher and an accomplished fiddler. He passed his love of music on to Dolly's mother and her siblings.

THE STORY BEHIND "I Will Always Love You"

"That song was so very personal to me. I wrote that song about my leaving *The Porter Wagoner Show*. Porter was having such a hard time with that because we had agreed that I would work with him for five years; I stayed for seven. But I was just trying to make him understand that I appreciated everything [that he had done], and I would always love him. And I wasn't leaving for any other reason other than I had my life to get on with, and I had other dreams and other things that I wanted to do with my life.

"He was having a hard time with that. And I thought, 'Well, you write songs. And you're not getting anywhere trying to talk to him. He's not listening. He won't hear you.' And so out of a very heavy heart and a very emotional time I wrote that song. And of course it meant a great deal to me. But then Whitney Houston took it and made it into something completely different. So I realized that people all over the world relate to it in different ways. Because I've had people say to me, 'Oh, we played that at my daddy's funeral.' Then somebody else would say they played it when they broke up with a partner. Somebody else would say it was when their children went off to college. So a song like that fits people in different ways. It makes you feel good to write a song like that for everybody."

—DOLLY PARTON

Dolly and Porter Wagoner backstage at the CMA Awards, 1975
PHOTO BY RAEANNE RUBENSTEIN

BACK *Through the Years*

All along, Dolly Parton's career has simultaneously looked backward for inspiration and leapt forward with new advances. So it's no surprise that she took a multi-dimensional approach to her historical legacy. In the last five years she's issued six books: two autobiographies, two children's books, a cookbook, and a best-selling work of fiction co-authored with James Patterson. In the same time span, she created a Netflix series, *Dolly Parton's Heartstrings*, that dramatized eight of her songs, and she produced or appeared in seven more specials on network TV and streaming channels.

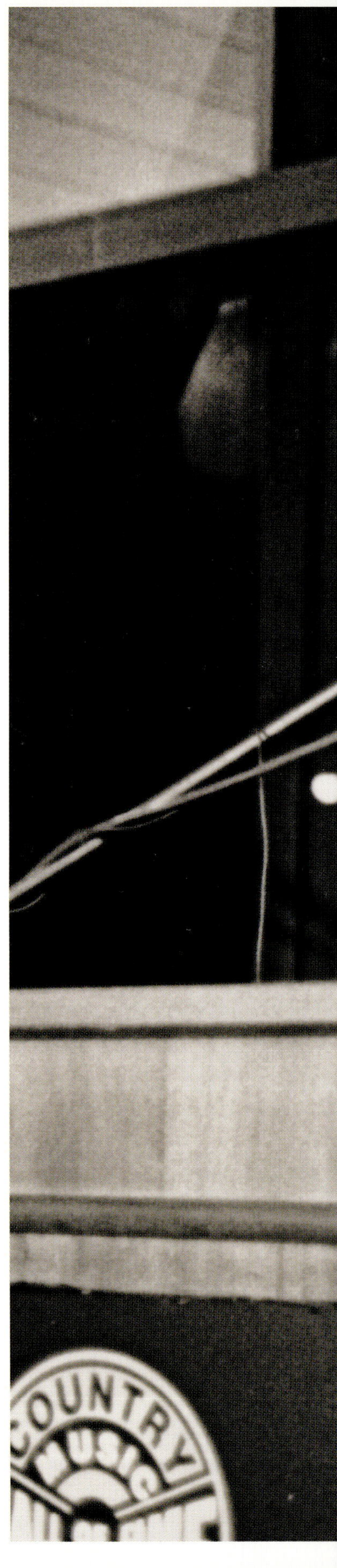

E. W. "Bud" Wendell with Dolly, who was elected to the Country Music Hall of Fame in 1999, at her Hall of Fame Medallion presentation. PHOTO BY BETH GWINN

COUNTRY
Honors
MUSIC
KENNEDY CENTER HONOR
DECEMBER 3, 2006
DOLLY PARTON

In 2019, a high-profile, nine-part podcast, *Dolly Parton's America*, widened her audience yet again. She's developing a stage musical based on her life story, has a museum on her life at Dollywood, and soon will have another museum in her new hotel under construction in downtown Nashville.

She is a member of the Nashville Songwriters Hall of Fame, the Songwriters Hall of Fame, the Rock & Roll Hall of Fame, and the Country Music Hall of Fame. She has received the National Medal of Arts and the Kennedy Center Honors.

Through it all, she has remained remarkably poised and down to earth. "I think I'm a star to everybody but me," Parton told *Southern Living* magazine. "I always wanted to be famous, but nobody could have thought of the extent it became. I'll see a whole wall of my pictures somewhere, and I'll wonder 'How did that happen?' It's more a joy than a surprise."

A custom Mitchell electric guitar, which Dolly played at her Rock & Roll Hall of Fame induction in 2022

OPPOSITE PAGE, CLOCKWISE FROM LEFT: Dolly wore this lamé top and fringed suede skirt, designed by Debra McGuire, for her induction into the Country Music Hall of Fame in 1999.

This Country Music Honors medallion from the CMA was presented to Dolly during the CMA's thirty-fifth anniversary TV show, *A Country Celebration*, January 1993.

This rainbow ribbon necklace with engraved bars was presented to Dolly at the Kennedy Center Honors in 2006.

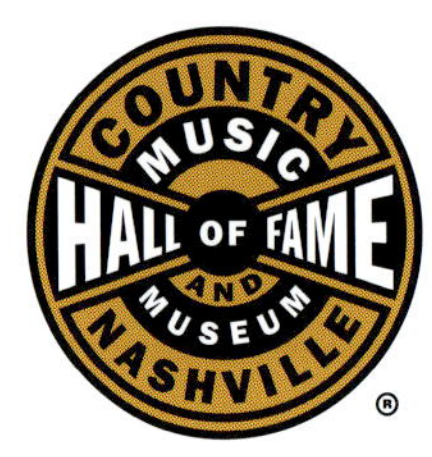

2025 BOARD OF OFFICERS AND TRUSTEES

TRUSTEES

OFFICERS

TRUSTEES EMERITI

LEGAL COUNSEL

CIRCLE GUARD

The Country Music Hall of Fame and Museum Circle Guard unites and celebrates individuals who have given their time, talent, and treasure to safeguard the integrity of country music and make it accessible to a global audience through the Museum. The Circle Guard designation ranks as the grandest distinction afforded to those whose unwavering commitment to the Museum protects the legacies of the members of the Country Music Hall of Fame, and, by extension, the time-honored achievements of all who are part of the country music story.

2025 GUARD

Steve Turner, Founder (1947–2025)

Kyle Young, Commander General

David Conrad

Bill Denny

Ken Levitan

Mary Ann McCready

Mike Milom

Jay Orr

Ken Roberts (1932–2022)

Seab Tuck

Jerry B. Williams

Jody Williams

Dolly in Nashville's Centennial Park, 1975. PHOTO BY RAEANNE RUBENSTEIN